Ripley's
Believe It or Not!®

The Collection VOL. IV

Matchstick

DRAGON

A MATCHSTICK MARVEL!

272,000	11	1,000	9 GAL
MATCHSTICKS	MONTHS	HOURS	OF GLUE

This matchstick model is an automated two-headed dragon that uses motion sensors to activate the moving wings as the mouths light up and roar! Known for his dozens of elaborate matchstick creations, Patrick Acton, of Gladbrook, Iowa, has created seven matchstick models for Ripley's including an International Space Station, a castle, and a steampunk train. On average, Acton completes one model per year for Ripley's, so stay tuned for what's next!

CIGARETTE LIGHTERS, which were invented in 1816, were developed **BEFORE MATCHES** were in 1826!

Inflated

WAS IT SOMETHING I ATE?

COW

COW

DEER

NOT YOUR TYPICAL BALLOON ANIMALS!

Hungarian artist Szollosi Geza creates unique animal art using animal skins and taxidermist's sewing techniques to create mounts as light as balloons. Geza's art generates responses from amused smiles to loud laughs.

TAXIDERMY

WE'RE HAVING A BALL!

COW

WILD BOAR

COW DENTURES?!
Dairy cows fitted with dentures can chew longer than cows with regular teeth—so they produce more milk!

Wild hogs can **DETECT SMELLS** up to 7 miles away or 25 feet underground!

DOG HAIR *Art*

BEAUTY IS IN THE EYE OF THE SHEAR-HOLDER

Jean Ford of Orlando, Florida is a commercial artist that turned professional dog groomer. Combining skills of both professions, Jean has created truly unique and bizarre portraits of her two pet spaniels using their own shaved hair!

Did you know that both cats' and dogs' noses **ARE UNIQUE** like human **FINGERPRINTS?**

NO HAIRCUT NEEDED!

Some dogs have hair instead of fur, such as: Bearded Collies, Lhasa Apsos, Coton de Tulear, Havanese, Tibetan Terriers, Maltese, Shih Tzus, and Yorkshire Terriers. Hair on these dogs won't shed and will keep growing until it dies or it's cut.

Kinetic
MEGALODON

This Megalodon kinetic sculpture is part submarine and part spaceship, teeming with the activity of its robotic crew. Artist Nemo Gould salvaged an F-94 bomber plane wing fuel tank and handcrafted and collected thousands of objects, from soup spoons to aircraft parts, to create this intricate grand miniature.

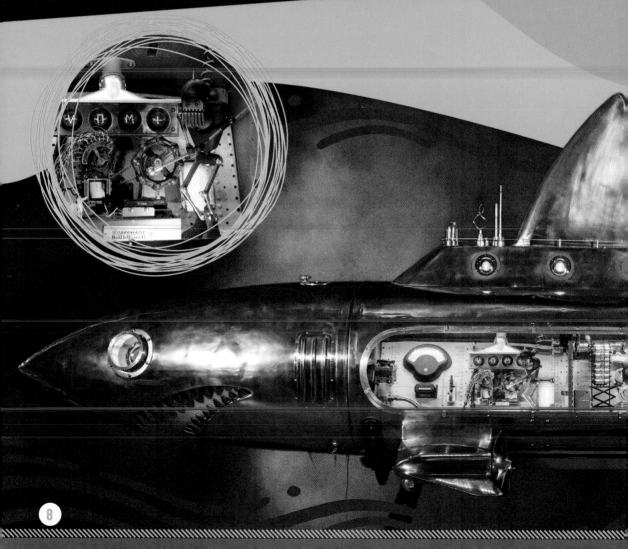

LARGEST SHARK EVER

The Megalodon, an ancient shark species that once ruled the seas, was the size of a bus and had teeth the size of a person's fist!

F-94 BOMBER fuel tank!

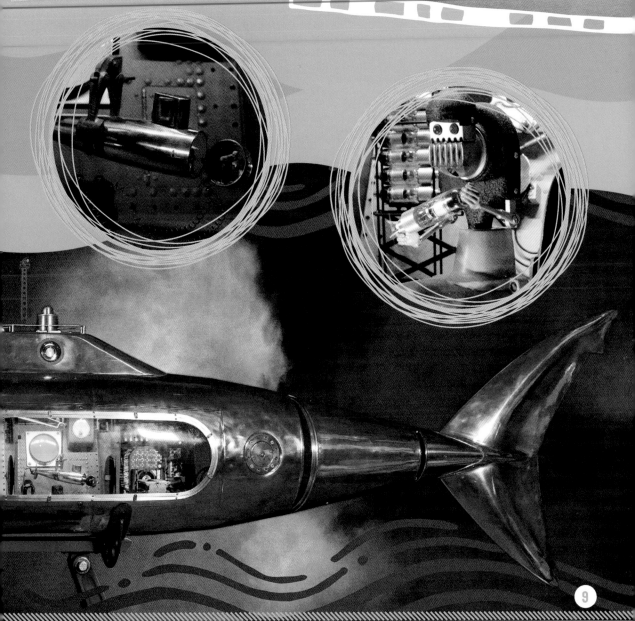

Beatles

MOSAIC GUITAR

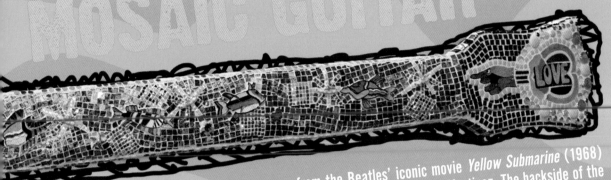

A vibrant mosaic portraying characters and scenes from the Beatles' iconic movie *Yellow Submarine* (1968) decorates this giant ten-foot long Gibson Les Paul guitar hand-crafted by Juliana Martinez. The backside of the guitar features a painting of Captain Fred and the Fab Four. **WE ALL LIVE IN A YELLOW SUBMARINE...**

Car Hood

The Beatles were **THE FIRST** to include the rock'n'roll **"DEVIL HORNS"** on an album cover.

Baby You Can
DRIVE MY CAR

Using grinders and metal knife blades, Michael Stodola of Wisconsin, USA, **ETCHED PORTRAITS** of Beatles John Lennon and Paul McCartney into the **CAR HOODS** of Volkswagen Beetles! **BELIEVE IT OR NOT!**

SILVERWARE sculpture

Shupe also sculpted a horse made from **10,000** pieces of **SILVER SPOONS.**

REAL MERMAIDS?!?

People who sail the oceans have always told fabulous stories of beautiful mermaids who lived under the waves. Believe It or Not!, the great showman P.T. Barnum once exhibited a creature like the one below, claiming it to be a genuine mermaid! Thousands of people paid 25 cents in 1842 to see P.T. Barnum's "Fiji Mermaid". Barnum insisted this "mermaid" was authentic until in his old age, he admitted it was just an ingenious fusing of the upper half of a monkey and the lower half of a fish!

ROBERT RIPLEY is seen here holding a **FIJI MERMAID!**

LOOKING SHARP!

Created by award-winning artist Eric Shupe of High Springs, Florida, this mermaid sculpture is made from over 10,000 silver knives and her hair is made from uncoiled telephone cables. Shupe collects the cutlery from restaurants, garage sales, and auctions, and his neighbors even leave donations on his front porch.

SAYS WHO?!!

In 2012, the National Ocean Service, a U.S. Government agency, officially declared that mermaids definitely don't exist!

13

TEAK WOOD *Sports Car*

WOOD YOU LIKE A RIDE?

Made in Indonesia entirely from teak wood, this scale model of the BUGATTI Veyron is based on one of the most famed and luxurious sports cars ever made, with a 1000- horsepower engine capable of speeds up to 254 miles per hour.

WORLD'S MOST EXPENSIVE AUTO

The 1931 Bugatti Royale exhibited at the New York International Antiques Show in 1987 and was valued at $8,100,000.

FAMOUS BUGATTI OWNERS

Tom Cruise	Cristiano Ronaldo	Flo Rida
Chris Brown	Katie Price	Xzibit
Jay-Z	Soulja Boy	The Game
Lil Wayne	Ralph Lauren	Scott Storch
Tom Brady	Floyd Mayweather Jr.	Birdman
Jay Leno	Criss Angel	Craig Jackson
Simon Cowell	T-Pain	

Ripley's has numerous **WOOD-CARVED VEHICLES** in The Collection including a Vespa, Testarossi Ferrari, motorcycle, wood boat FIAT, JAGUAR, pumpkin carriage, Mercedes-Benz, and Ferrari.

DRAGON PEOPLE

The people of China have a long-held belief that they are descendents of the dragon, a tradition that is firmly embedded in their culture and one that is encountered across all aspects of Chinese society and in the minds of its people.

龍

The Chinese symbol for **DRAGON**

Chinese
METAL DRAGON

9FT **X 20**FT **3,000**
TALL   LONG   LBS

THAT'S SOME HEAVY METAL!
Often symbolizing the emperor in Chinese art, Asian dragons were believed to be benevolent, spiritual creatures that were teachers in art and magic.

Rx-ELLENT!

Dinosaur bones uncovered by Chinese villagers are believed to be dragon bones and are ground up into traditional medicine!

Paper DRESSES

READY TO ROLL?

These brides certainly are, in dresses made completely from toilet paper! The lacework, the intricate designs, the ruffles: 100% TP. Looking absolutely Charmin, these dresses were finalists in the Cheap-Chic Weddings contest with a grand prize of $10,000!

The Finnish cellphone company NOKIA, founded in 1865, used to **MAKE TOILET PAPER!**

PASSING NOTES

These dresses are the creation of fashion design student Dien Nguyen and are made of hundreds of sticky notes. Nguyen was inspired by the rainbow when designing these creative paper wearables.

The most **EXPENSIVE DRESS** in the world is the "Happy Birthday" dress worn by **MARILYN MONROE** while she sang "Happy Birthday" to president JFK. The dress was purchased at auction by Ripley's in 2016.

ISLAND RECORDS

Actual broken records are assembled here in this portrait of Bob Marley as a tribute to his more-than 20 million records sold during and after his life.

Kate Middleton was the **FIRST COMMONER** to marry a prince close to the British Throne in **350 YEARS!**

GREEN QUEEN

This portrait of Princess Catherine, made from lost and found objects, makes a statement about how world leaders can influence citizens all around the globe to use their resources wisely. Waste not, Want not!

There are **TEN TYPES** of soda cans in this pop-culture portrait!

POP ART

This super portrait of one of the hottest heroes in current pop culture is made out of thousands of strips of colored soda pop cans.

UNBELIEVABLE
Art

A ROSE BY ANY OTHER NAME

A saint who dedicated her life to helping the poverty-stricken, Mother Teresa has been painted on white roses, which fittingly represent innocence and purity.

Ripley's collection of art showcases not just the "fine," but the imaginitive, quirky, and unique. An array of human ingenuity is showcased in these peculiar portraits. You'll never believe what these art pieces are made of!

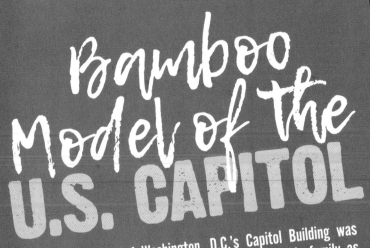

Bamboo Model of the U.S. CAPITOL

This scale model of Washington, D.C.'s Capitol Building was made by Vietnamese immigrant Linh Vuong and his family as a testimony to their patriotism. Lighting up with red and blue, this model was made entirely from slivers of bamboo thinner than common toothpicks! There is very little glue; almost all the pieces have been attached by threading them through small holes meticulously drilled by hand, taking over a year to complete!

10FT **X 9**FT
LONG   WIDE

150
LBS

1 MILLON
BAMBOO SLIVERS

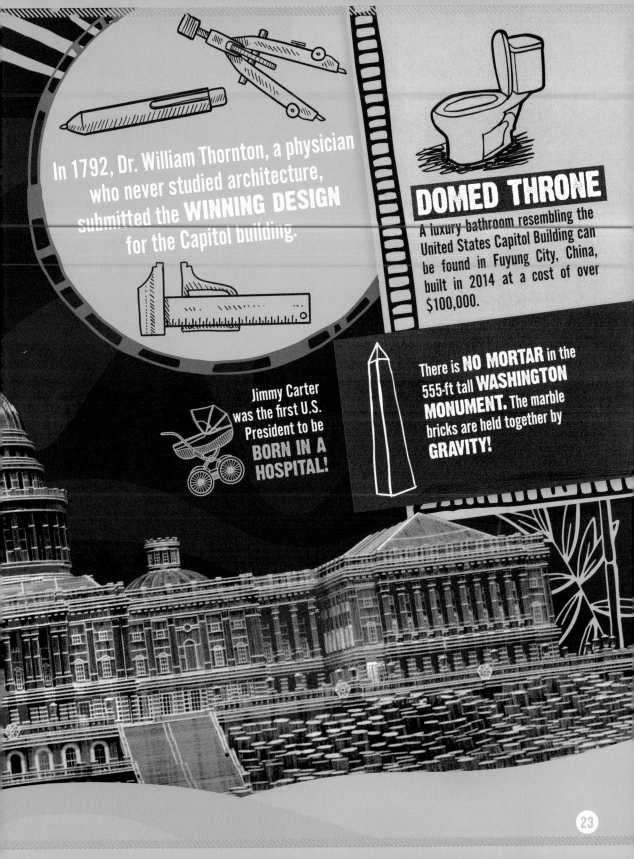

In 1792, Dr. William Thornton, a physician who never studied architecture, submitted the **WINNING DESIGN** for the Capitol building.

DOMED THRONE

A luxury bathroom resembling the United States Capitol Building can be found in Fuyung City, China, built in 2014 at a cost of over $100,000.

Jimmy Carter was the first U.S. President to be **BORN IN A HOSPITAL!**

There is **NO MORTAR** in the 555-ft tall **WASHINGTON MONUMENT.** The marble bricks are held together by **GRAVITY!**

GENUINE Shrunken Heads

TROPHY HEADS

In Ecuador, South America, the Jivaroan tribes were known for severing the heads of their enemies in battle, removing the skull, and shrinking the skin to fist-size as part of religious ceremonies. These trophy heads, called Tsantsas, were worn or displayed to ward off the vengeful spirits of their owners. In the early 1900s, the tourist trade for Tsantsas sharply increased "head-hunting" until the local governments banned the head-trade.

ROBERT RIPLEY acquired his first genuine shrunken head in Lima, Peru, in 1923. Today, there are **MORE THAN 100** shrunken heads in the Ripley collection!

Ripley's has the **LARGEST** shrunken head collection in the world!

>> HOW TO << SHRINK A HEAD

1 Remove the skull from the rest of the body.

2 Make an incision from the neck to the top of the head. Peel the skin back and remove the cranium.

3 Sew up the skin, close the eyes, and seal the mouth shut with vines and wood pins.

4 Hold the head upside-down and fill it with hot rocks and sand.

5 Boil the head in water containing herbs and tannins for about three days.

6 When the head shrinks to the size of a fist, rub the skin with ashes and hold it over a smoking fire to harden and darken it.

7 Decorate with beads, feathers, and beetle wings.

TRIBAL & PRIMITIVE
Artifacts

Animal votive skulls are cherished as **RELIGIOUS RELICS** by Lamaist monks in Tibet.

HUMAN SKIN MASK

DANCE MASK

EXOTIC ARTIFACTS

Fascinated with foreign cultures and customs, Robert Ripley traveled to the most remote parts of world collecting artifacts from indigenous tribal peoples of New Guinea, Fiji, Peru, the Congo, Kenya, China, India, the Easter Islands, and above the Arctic Circle. His revelations changed how Westerners viewed the world.

CAN I MASK YOU A QUESTION??

WOOD YOU CUT IT OUT!

TRIBAL MASKS

THE PIRAHA TRIBE OF BRAZIL HAS ALMOST **NO WORDS** FOR COUNTING, COLORS, TIME, OR RELATIONSHIPS. **SAY WHAT?!**

FANTASY COFFIN

The Ga people of Ghana, West Africa, bury their family members in elaborate, often sculptural, coffins that celebrate their profession or reflect their social status. They believe the afterlife continues on similar to life on Earth and that ancestors have great influence on the living. Family members treat the deceased with great respect to ensure their sympathy and goodwill.

PRANKS
of Nature

Robert Ripley referred to genetically mutated animals as "pranks of nature," displaying some of the most unusual animals ever seen. From two-headed parrots to one-eyed lambs, Ripley's pranks of nature can be found at every Odditorium around the world.

6-LEGGED BABY GOAT

THEY SAY TWO HEADS ARE BETTER THAN ONE!

Parrot populations can develop **LOCAL DIALECTS** in their songs depending on what birds they grew up with!

Both trunks were **TOTALLY FUNCTIONAL**, helping the elephant live a normal life!

Do you notice what's **MISSING?!**

Officials in Indonesia have trained elephants to help control forest fires!

ELE-FACTS:

Some elephants have been seen **BURYING THEIR DEAD** and returning to visit those gravesites generations later.

An **ELEPHANT'S TRUNK** is made up of about 100,000 muscles, but **NO BONES**!

ALBINOS are pure white animals with lack of skin pigment and **PINK** eyes.

LEUCISTIC ANIMALS

are white animals with **BLUE** eyes. Ripley's has both in their Zoological Collection!

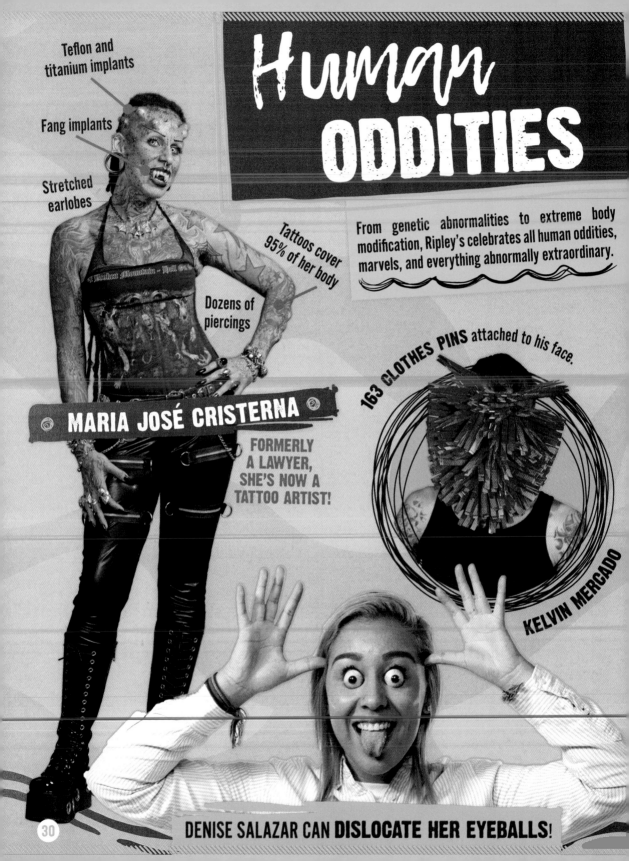

Human ODDITIES

Teflon and titanium implants

Fang implants

Stretched earlobes

Tattoos cover 95% of her body

Dozens of piercings

From genetic abnormalities to extreme body modification, Ripley's celebrates all human oddities, marvels, and everything abnormally extraordinary.

MARIA JOSÉ CRISTERNA

FORMERLY A LAWYER, SHE'S NOW A TATTOO ARTIST!

163 CLOTHES PINS attached to his face.

KELVIN MERCADO

DENISE SALAZAR CAN **DISLOCATE HER EYEBALLS!**

ROBERT WADLOW

Robert Wadlow, the tallest man to have ever lived, came from a "normal" sized family in Alton, Illinois. People stared wherever he went, which made him quiet, shy, and sensitive to his size—as one could imagine!

HEIGHT
8 FT 11 IN
WEIGHT
440 LBS

Paduang women of Myanmar **STRETCH** their **NECKS** as much as 18 inches with brass rings. A ring is added annually until the total number of rings reaches 25!

Women from the Sara Tribe in Chad, Africa, insert **WOODEN PLATES** into their mouths, extending their lips to **EXTREME PROPORTIONS**.

KHAGENDRA MAGAR

Khagendra Magar of Nepal is fully grown at 22 inches. His growth was stunted by a pituitary gland disorder, but that doesn't stop him from doing his favorite things, like dancing and karate.

HEIGHT
22 IN
WEIGHT
10 LBS

THE INCREDIBLE
Robert Ripley

THE MOST INTERESTING MAN IN THE WORLD!

Searching for oddities in over 200 countries, Ripley wowed the world daily with his publications read by more than 80 million people! His collections of unique artifacts and previously untold stories of the customs and beliefs of cultures all over the globe fill 32 Ripley's Odditoriums in 11 countries. He explored the far corners of the earth for 35 years, and his adventures truly brought together the largest collection of oddities in the world representing the human experience.

An UNBELIEVABLE Life

1918	1922	1929	1933

A CARTOONIST
The cartoon *Champs and Chumps* debuts in the *New York Globe* as Ripley's first collection of odd facts and feats.

AN ADVENTURER
Ripley's dream of traveling the world comes true when he lands an assignment to search for new material in Asia.

AN AUTHOR
Ripley's 1st book, a collection of cartoons and essays, is published. He became the author of five books!

A COLLECTOR
The first Odditorium opens at the World's Fair in Chicago, bringing in two million people.

Has a star on the
Hollywood Walk of Fame.

Called "The Modern Marco Polo."

First cartoonist to
earn a million dollars.

Semi-pro baseball player.

Voted the most popular
man in America in 1936.

On-location live broadcast.

1930–1944

1949

1950

A RADIO PERSONALITY
Ripley hosts a wildly successful weekly radio show, being the first to broadcast from underground, underwater, and from the sky (in a falling parachute)!

A TV SHOW HOST
The weekly television show features Ripley displaying his artifacts, drawing cartoons, re-enacting stories, and interviewing the "stars" of the stories.

A LEGACY
After Ripley's death in 1949, entrepreneur John Arthur buys Ripley's artifacts collection and opens the first permanent Odditorium in St. Augustine, Florida.

CAN YOU COUNT THE ELEPHANT'S LEGS?

Wind your way through the

JUNGLE MAZE

START

FINISH

What's your BAND NAME?

Use the first letter of your first name for column **#1** and the last letter of your last name for column **#2** to find out!

#1	#2
A – Abnormal	A – Almonds
B – Bearded	B – Berries
C – Creepy	C – Carriages
D – Domesticated	D – Dragons
E – Eleven	E – Elephants
F – Forty	F – Furs
G – Gold	G – Goats
H – Hopping	H – Hoagies
I – Iridescent	I – Icebergs
J – Jumping	J – Jelly Beans
K – Kangaroo	K – Kings
L – Little	L – Lizards
M – Magnificent	M – Megalodon
N – Nine	N – Nunchucks
O – Orange	O – Octopus
P – Pickled	P – Puppies
Q – Quaint	Q – Queens
R – Red	R – Ribbons
S – Silver	S – Scales
T – Twisted	T – Taxidermists
U – Under	U – Ulcers
V – Venomous	V – Vampire
W – Wild	W – Weapon
X – Xeroxed	X – Xenons
Y – Yellow	Y – Yodels
Z – Zippered	Z – Zombies

WORD SEARCH

Find these words:
ANCIENT
TEAK
ART
DRAGON
WEDDING
MEGALODON
GUITAR
SHRUNKEN
TAXIDERMY
MERMAID

```
R Y V X T A N C I E N T
N V V Y R X P I V Q X E X
V T M Y W O S J D C K D
Y N O D O L A G E M N D
E M W W Q P U Z H H U R
D X R Y E I T D G Y R A
W K A E T D I R H V H G
L T P A D A D E A W S O
H X R Y M I X I S K F N
P B D R A S X N N O O A
C U E F A J B A J G C W
Y M V J F P G M T Y K Y
```

FACT or FIB?

Determine which statement in each pair is NOT true. Clues can be found throughout this book!

MEGALODON
a. Megalodon is the largest shark that ever lived.
b. The Megalodon's tooth was about the size of a person's femur.

DRAGONS
a. The Chinese believe that cats are the decendants of dragons.
b. Dinosaur bones discovered by Chinese villagers are traditionally believed to be dragon bones and are ground up into medicines.

WASHINGTON D.C.
a. The winning design for the Capitol was submitted in 1792 by Dr. William Thornton.
b. George Washington built the Washington Monument, mortaring each brick together.

MERMAIDS
a. P.T. Barnum showcased his Fiji Mermaid in 1842 for an admission price of 25 cents.
b. The National Ocean Service, a U.S. Government agency, declared that mermaids do exist.

THE BEATLES
a. Were the first to include the rock 'n' roll "devil horns" on an album cover.
b. Were in a movie called Blue Submarine in 1968.

ROBERT RIPLEY
a. His travels took him to the most remote parts of the world collecting artifacts.
b. Robert Ripley did not travel farther north than the Arctic Circle.

CROSSWORD FUN

Use the clues below to solve this puzzle.
HINT: The book can help you find the solution!

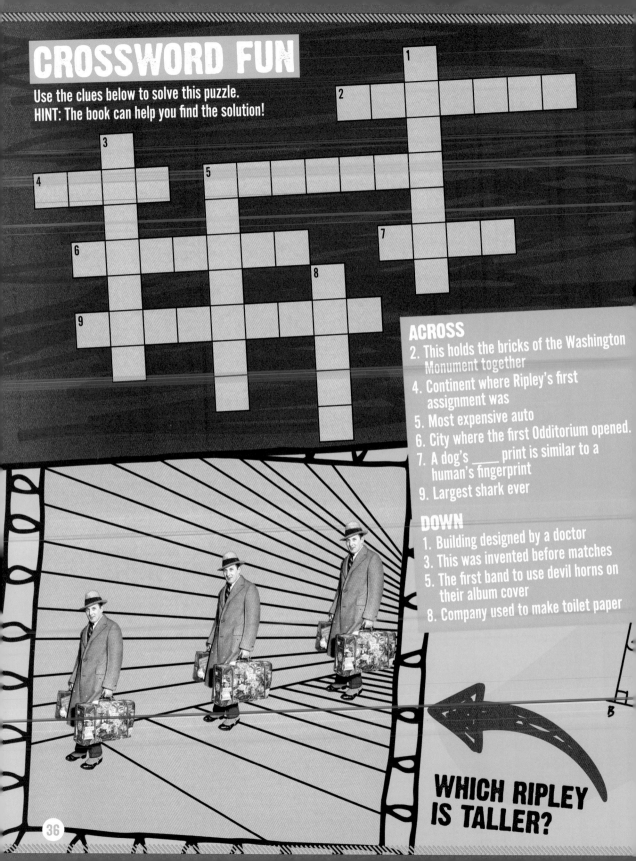

ACROSS
2. This holds the bricks of the Washington Monument together
4. Continent where Ripley's first assignment was
5. Most expensive auto
6. City where the first Odditorium opened.
7. A dog's _____ print is similar to a human's fingerprint
9. Largest shark ever

DOWN
1. Building designed by a doctor
3. This was invented before matches
5. The first band to use devil horns on their album cover
8. Company used to make toilet paper

WHICH RIPLEY IS TALLER?

WORD SCRAMBLE

Unscramble these words related to Robert Ripley.

HEUVREATOR

COTOCELRL

IUDTRDCKOI

IAORD

WRLDO

UTAHRO

RNLVEA

OSIOTHRCTA

OXLREEP

WHAT the WHAT?

These triangles have the same parts **BUT**...

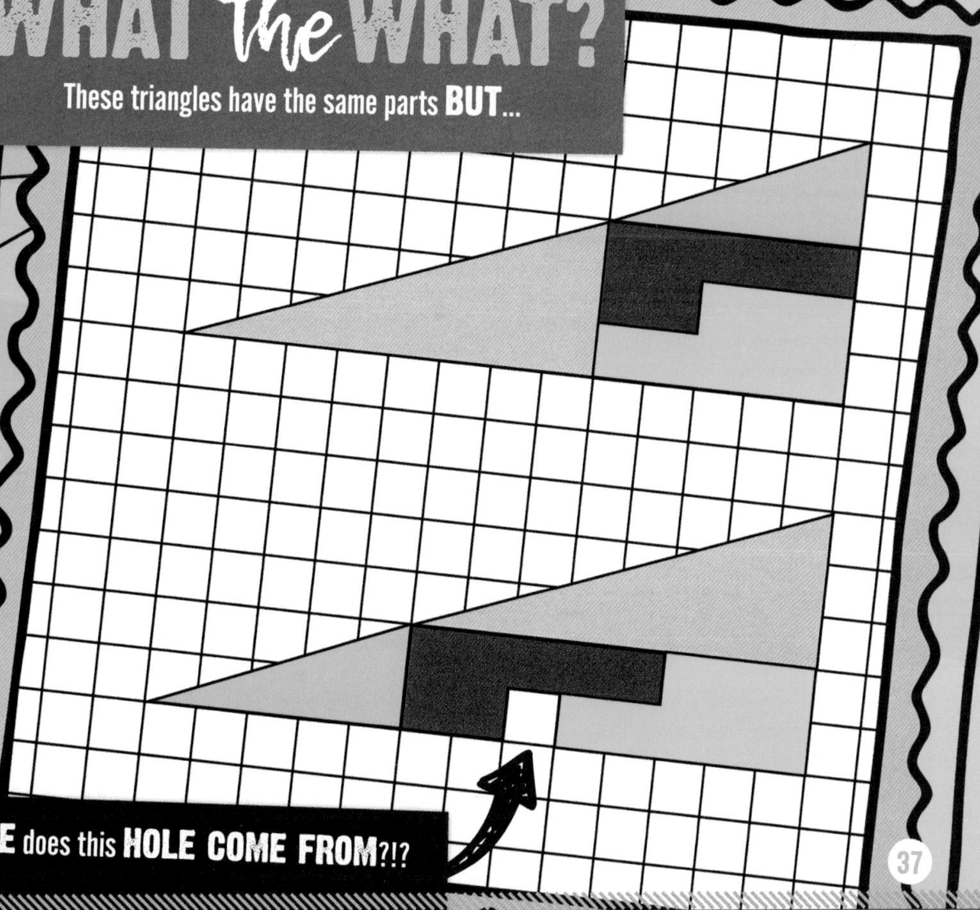

...**WHERE** does this **HOLE COME FROM**?!?

CA ∥ HG

$A\hat{C}B = \frac{2}{5}$

Legendary African
FERTILITY STATUES

In 1993, Ripley's acquired two authentic African fertility statues carved by Baule tribesmen from the Ivory Coast sometime in the 1930s. Believed to have the power to help women become pregnant with a simple touch, these 70 pound ebony statues have traveled the world since 1996, visiting every Odditorium—and Ripley's has collected thousands of letters from women confirming statue-assisted births, including Ripley's employees and some who were told it was impossible! These statues have been featured on 50 different television shows in 20 countries, including *Unsolved Mysteries*.

See the video about the Fertility Statues' success stories!
RIPLEYS.COM/FERTILITY-STATUES

THE SCIENCE OF
RIPLEY'S
BELIEVE IT
OR NOT!®

Explore remarkable realms of extreme biology and weird wonders of the world as the unbelievable is scientifically illuminated through challenges, experiments, touchable artifacts and multimedia interactives.

SCIENCE WORLD
Vancouver, British Columbia
Fall 2017

SPRINGS PRESERVE
Las Vegas, NV
Jan. 27–May 7, 2017

**INDIANAPOLIS
CHILDREN'S MUSEUM**
Indianapolis, IN
May 26–Sept. 4, 2018

DISCOVERY PLACE INC.
Charlotte, NC
May 26–Sept. 4, 2017

EXPLORATION PLACE
Wichita, KS
May 26–Sept. 3, 2019

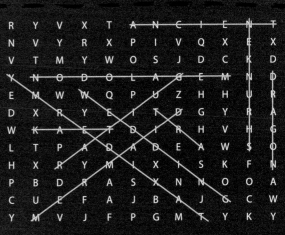

ACTIVITY ANSWERS:

ELEPHANT LEGS: You're seeing more legs than you should, because the elephant's feet have been erased and redrawn in the space between the legs.

FACT OR FIB: b, a, b, b, b, b

CROSSWORD: 1-Capitol, 2-Gravity, 3-Lighter, 4-Asia, 5-Beatles, 6-Chicago, 7-Nose, 8-Nokia, 9-Megalodon

WHICH IS TALLER? They're all the same size!

WORD SCRAMBLE: Collector, Radio, Author, Cartoonist, Adventurer, Odditorium, World, Travel, Explore

WHAT THE WHAT? Examine where the 2 hypotenuse intersect the grid. The bottom triangle intersects the grid higher on the x-axis than the top triangle does. This extra area is equivalent to the area of one grid square.

```
R  Y  V  X  T  A  N  C  I  E  N  T
N  V  Y  R  X  P  I  V  Q  X  E  X
V  T  M  Y  W  O  S  J  D  C  K  D
Y  N  O  D  O  L  A  G  E  M  N  D
E  M  W  W  Q  P  U  Z  H  U  R  R
D  X  R  Y  E  I  T  D  G  Y  R  A
W  K  A  E  T  D  I  R  H  V  H  G
L  T  P  A  D  A  D  E  A  W  S  O
H  X  R  Y  M  I  X  I  S  K  F  N
P  B  D  R  A  S  Y  N  N  O  O  A
C  U  E  F  A  J  B  A  J  G  C  W
Y  M  V  J  F  P  G  M  T  Y  K  Y
```

ODDITORIUMS
Around the World

Copenhagen
[Denmark]

1

2

Blackpool
London
[United Kingdom]

2

Cavendish, PEI
Niagara Falls
[Canada]

18

1

Amsterdam
[Netherlands]

3

Guadalajara
Mexico City
Veracruz
[Mexico]

U.S.A.

Atlantic City, NJ	New York, NY
Baltimore, MD	Ocean City, MD
Branson, MO	Orlando, FL
Gatlinburg, TN	Panama City Beach, FL
Grand Prairie, TX	San Antonio, TX
Hollywood, CA	San Francisco, CA
Key West, FL	St. Augustine, FL
Myrtle Beach, SC	Williamsburg, VA
Newport, OR	Wisconsin Dells, WI

SUBMIT YOUR BION!

We are always searching for the latest in the weird
and unusual. Send us your Believe It or Not stories!

RIPLEYS.COM/SUBMISSIONS